PRIDE

A DICTIONARY FOR THE VAIN

Aadamsmedia
Avon, Massachusetts

Published by
Adams Media, a division of F+W Media, Inc.
57 Littlefield Street, Avon, MA 02322. U.S.A.
www.adamsmedia.com

ISBN 10: 1-4405-2770-9
ISBN 13: 978-1-4405-2770-8
eISBN 10: 1-4405-2823-3
eISBN 13: 978-1-4405-2823-1

Printed in the United States of America.

10 9 8 7 6 5 4 3 2 1

Library of Congress Cataloging-in-Publication Data
is available from the publisher.

This publication is designed to provide accurate and authoritative
information with regard to the subject matter covered. It is sold
with the understanding that the publisher is not engaged in
rendering legal, accounting, or other professional advice. If legal
advice or other expert assistance is required, the services of a
competent professional person should be sought.
—From a *Declaration of Principles* jointly adopted
by a Committee of the American Bar Association
and a Committee of Publishers and Associations

Many of the designations used by manufacturers and sellers to
distinguish their product are claimed as trademarks. Where
those designations appear in this book and Adams Media was
aware of a trademark claim, the designations have been printed
with initial capital letters.

Interior illustration © clipart.com

This book is available at quantity discounts for bulk purchases.
For information, please call 1-800-289-0963.

An Introduction to
Pride

pride

(*pryd*)

NOUN: An inordinate opinion of one's own
superiority.

Hubris blinds those so taken with themselves that
they often fall from the heights their own vanity
builds. No matter the cause—be it like Gatsby's
great wealth on the West Egg or Lucifer's charm
in *Paradise Lost*—the outcome never favors those
only full of themselves. The desire to champion
their own greatness ultimately proves to be their
greatest weakness. This flaw in the self-perceived
flawlessness of the prideful leaves nothing to boast
about but plenty from which to learn. While pride is
defined best in the reflection of any aspiring Narcissus, this impressive dictionary captures the essence
of the most vainglorious sin.

A

❧

accentuate

(*ak-SEN-choo-ayt*)

VERB: To intensify or accent. To *accentuate* something is to emphasize or stress it. To strengthen or heighten the effect of something is to *accentuate* it.

achievement

(*uh-CHEEV-muhnt*)

NOUN: An accomplishment, something done with skill.

acuity

(*uh-KYOO-ih-tee*)

NOUN: Penetrating, sharp intelligence.

acumen

(*uh-KYOO-muhn*)

NOUN: Keenness of judgment. *Acumen* refers to an ability to make quick, accurate decisions and evaluations. It is characterized by rapid discernment and insight.

ad nauseam

(*ad NAW-zee-uhm*)

NOUN: To a sickening degree. This Latin phrase often is invoked when someone goes on and on about something and just doesn't know when to stop.

adamant

(*AD-uh-muhnt*)

NOUN: Unwilling to submit; stubborn and unyielding. Historically, *adamant* refers to a legendary stone of infinite hardness. (The word *diamond* shares the same root.)

adept

(*uh-DEPT*)

NOUN: Proficient; expert; highly skilled. *Adept* refers to someone who is very good at performing a given task.

> *The young artist believed himself quite the Michelangelo: as ADEPT with paint as he was with stone.*

adhere

(*ad-HEER*)

VERB: Hold fast to, usually with a sense of honor or allegiance.

adherent

(*ad-HEER-uhnt*)

ADJECTIVE: Describes one who is devoted to or strongly associated with a cause or opinion.

Pride is seldom delicate:

it will please itself with very

mean advantages.

—Samuel Johnson

admire

(*ad-MY-uhr*)

VERB: To feel admiration or respect for someone or something.

adore

(*uh-DOHR*)

VERB: To love deeply or intensely.

Narcissus ADORED in himself what he should have loved in others.

adrenaline

(*uh-DREN-l-in*)

NOUN: A chemical produced in the body that gives one added strength and energy; epinephrine.

adulate

(*AJ-uh-layt*)

VERB: Flatter or praise excessively or obsequiously.

adulation

(*AJ-uh-lay-shuhn*)

NOUN: Extreme praise, admiration, or flattery, especially of a servile nature. *Adulation* is generally taken to describe acclaim and admiration that is out of scope with its object.

Edmund Spenser's epic poem, The Faerie Queen, *was an extended ADULATION that flattered Queen Elizabeth I.*

affection
(*uh-FEK-shuhn*)
NOUN: A positive, fond feeling. Also, the physical display of these feelings.

aficionado
(*uh-fish-yuh-NAH-doh*)
NOUN: A devotee, someone who is enthralled with and supports a particular activity. The writer Ernest Hemingway helped to popularize this word of Spanish origin.

aggrandize
(*uh-GRAN-dyz*)
VERB: To raise the importance of or make to appear great. To *aggrandize* is to increase the prestige, influence, reputation, or power of a person or institution.

airs and graces
(*airz and GRAY-zuhs*)
NOUN: Displaying superiority, often falsely.

aloof
(*uh-LOOF*)
ADJECTIVE: Indifferent or uninterested; unsociable.

amoral
(*ay-MAWR-uhl*)
NOUN: Without moral discretion or standards. To be *amoral* is to act as though the distinctions of right and wrong are nonexistent. A person who is *amoral* is neither moral nor immoral.

amour propre
(*uh-moor PRAW-pruh*)
NOUN: French for self-esteem, this term means excessive self-worth.

apotheosis
(*uh-poth-ee-OH-sis*)
NOUN: A perfect example; the epitome of a person, place, thing, etc. Also, *apotheosis* can mean something or someone elevated to godlike status.

ardent
(*AHR-dnt*)
ADJECTIVE: Intense, passionate, devoted; characterized by high emotion. *Ardent* people show great enthusiasm for causes and people close to them.

aristocratic
(*uh-ris-tuh-KRAT-ik*)
ADJECTIVE: Grand and stylish.

arrogance

(*AYR-uh-guhns*)

NOUN: A display of exaggerated self-worth.

The general's ARROGANCE led him to believe he could overtake the opposing army even though he was outmanned twenty to one.

arrogant

(*AYR-uh-guhnt*)

ADJECTIVE: Having an exaggerated sense of self-worth, displaying a sense of unwarranted importance.

assumption of superiority

(*uh-SUHMP-shuhn ov suh-peer-ee-AWR-ih-tee*)

PHRASE: A condescending attitude that implies disdain.

assumptive

(*uh-SUHMP-tiv*)

ADJECTIVE: Excessively forward and presumptuous.

assurance

(*uh-SHOOR-uhns*)

NOUN: Convincing someone of something in order to give confidence, or confidence in one's own abilities.

Pride is the mask of one's

own faults.

—JEWISH PROVERB

attitude

(*AT-ih-tood*)

NOUN: Presenting oneself with self-confidence.

Linden entered the room with such ATTITUDE that conversations fell to a hush.

august

(*aw-GUHST*)

ADJECTIVE: Impressive, venerable.

autoeroticism

(*aw-toh-ih-ROT-uh-siz-uhm*)

NOUN: Sexual excitement brought about by thinking or fantasizing about one's own body.

B

be stuck on oneself
(*bee stuhk awn wuhn-SELF*)
PHRASE: Full of conceit.

bearing
(*BAYR-ing*)
NOUN: The way someone stands or holds themselves.

benchmark
(*BENCH-mahrk*)
NOUN: A standard by which to measure; the exemplary performance or criterion.

biggety
(*BIG-ih-tee*)
ADJECTIVE: Boastful or self-important.

bighead
(*BIG-hed*)
NOUN: An arrogant person.

bigheaded
(*BIG-hed-ed*)
ADJECTIVE: To act as though you are a self-centered person.

bloated

(*BLOH-tid*)

ADJECTIVE: Swollen or enlarged.

The politician had such a BLOATED ego that he could not accept his second-place finish and called for a recount.

bloviate

(*BLOH-vee-eyt*)

VERB: To speak pompously and at great length.

blow one's own horn

(*bloh wuhnz ohn hawrn*)

PHRASE: To imply in speech that one thinks himself above others; to show arrogance.

blow one's own trumpet

(*bloh wuhnz ohn TRUHM-pit*)

PHRASE: See *blow one's own horn*.

blowhard

(*BLOH-hahrd*)

NOUN: Someone who is boastful in an unpleasant manner.

boast
(*bohst*)
VERB: As a verb this term means to show off and talk with excessive pride. It can also be used as a noun.

boastful
(*BOHST-fuhl*)
ADJECTIVE: Showing off and talking with excessive pride.

bold
(*bohld*)
ADJECTIVE: Confident and fearless.

boldness
(*BOHLD-nes*)
NOUN: The quality of being confident and fearless in an aggressive way.

bomb
(*bom*)
NOUN: The best; a good thing.

bombast

(*BOM-bast*)

NOUN: Haughty, overblown, or pompous talk or writing. Someone who engages in *bombast* indulges a taste for an exaggerated rhetorical style.

> *The critic's BOMBAST may have earned him a column in the literary magazine, but it never won him friends among its readers.*

bombastic

(*bom-BAS-tik*)

ADJECTIVE: Characterized by being haughty or overblown.

bovarist

(*BOH-vuh-rist*)

NOUN: Derived from Flaubert's arrogant lead character in the novel *Madame Bovary*, this means a person with a high view of oneself; conceited.

brag

(*brag*)

VERB: To boast.

braggadocio

(*brag-uh-DOH-shee-oh*)

NOUN: Bragging or meaningless boasting. *Braggadocio* can refer both to actual boasting or to a person who engages in it.

braggart

(*BRAG-ert*)

NOUN: A person who boasts.

When Michael took the podium, his colleagues knew to expect a detailed account of the BRAGGART'S many accomplishments.

bravado

(*bruh-VAH-doh*)

NOUN: An open show of bravery. That which is characterized by a display of boldness shows *bravado*.

brave

(*brayv*)

ADJECTIVE: Courageous, exhibiting courage.

brazen

(*BRAY-zuhn*)

ADJECTIVE: Bold or shameless in display; unconcerned with the reactions of others.

brazenfaced

(*BRAY-zuhn-fayst*)

ADJECTIVE: Shameless.

When a proud man hears

another praised, he feels

himself injured.

—ENGLISH PROVERB

brazenly

(*BRAY-zuhn-lee*)

ADVERB: Bold; unrestrained by convention.

bridle

(*BRYD-l*)

VERB: Turning down one's nose at something in disdain; as a noun it is headgear for a horse.

bull

(*bull*)

NOUN; VERB: In addition to the animal, this word has a number of meanings. As a noun, a *bull* is someone who buys stocks optimistically expecting a price rise. It also denotes a formal proclamation by the pope. As an adjective, *bull* means to act with force or to engage in idle, boastful talk.

> *Over the course of dinner, the young woman began to see right through the arrogant BULL her date was trying to have her believe.*

bull-rinky

(*bool-ringk-EE*)

NOUN: An antiquated way of saying "bullshit."

bullshitter

(*BOOL-shit-er*)

NOUN: A person who boasts, often in a way that is unwarranted.

bullshooter

(*BOOL-shoot-er*)

NOUN: An old-fashioned way of saying that some-one is a bullshitter.

bumptious

(*BUHMP-shuhs*)

ADJECTIVE: Overbearing or crudely assertive. Someone who is *bumptious* is overly pushy or impertinent.

bunk flying

(*buhngk FLY-ing*)

PHRASE: An American euphemism for boasting.

C

cat's meow

(*kats mee-OW*)

PHRASE: Another way of saying cat's pajamas.

cat's pajamas

(*kats puh-JAH-muhz*)

PHRASE: An outdated term meaning something or someone great or excellent.

cavalier

(*kav-uh-LEER*)

ADJECTIVE: To act in a way that shows a lack of respect or haughtiness.

> *Jamie's CAVALIER attitude helped her fit right in with the rest of the imperious debutantes.*

certitude

(*SUR-ti-tood*)

NOUN: An attitude of certainty or conviction.

charismatic

(*kar-iz-MAT-ik*)

ADJECTIVE: Possessing a special quality associated with leadership, authority, confidence, and overall personal appeal. While we generally use charismatic in reference to a person, the word also refers to certain Christian sects and ideas that emphasize demonstrative or ecstatic worship.

chauvinist

(*SHOH-vuh-nist*)

NOUN: A person who shows bias toward one's own group with the belief that that group is superior to all others.

cheeky

(*CHEE-kee*)

ADJECTIVE: Impudent and bold; insolent.

chestiness

(*ches-TEE-nes*)

NOUN: To display arrogance.

chutzpah

(*KHOOT-spuh*)

NOUN: Yiddish, meaning gall, audacity, impudence.

clever clogs

(*KLEV-er klogs*)

PHRASE: A British term meaning someone who is ostentatious and knowledgeable.

cock-a-hoop

(*KOK-uh-hoop*)

ADJECTIVE: Boastful and pleased regarding a triumph.

cock of the walk

(*kok ov thuh wawk*)

PHRASE: A person who dominates others in a group setting.

cocksure

(*KOK-shoor*)

ADJECTIVE: Extremely, swaggeringly confident; probably overconfident.

cocky

(*KOK-ee*)

ADJECTIVE: Boldly arrogant, derived from the confident manner of a male rooster.

commemorate

(*kuh-MEM-uh-rayt*)

VERB: To serve as a memorial for; to mark or celebrate as a significant event.

> *The overzealous king did not even wait for the war to officially end before commissioning a statue to COMMEMORATE his opponent's defeat.*

complacent

(*kuhm-PLAY-suhnt*)

NOUN: Satisfied with oneself; smug; content.

compliment
(*KOM-pluh-ment*)
VERB: To praise or flatter.

conceit
(*kuhn-SEET*)
NOUN: Pride in oneself.

conceited
(*kuhn-SEE-tid*)
ADJECTIVE: Excessively proud and vain.

condescending
(*kon-duh-SEN-ding*)
ADJECTIVE: To act in a manner that implies superiority.

confidence
(*KON-fi-duhns*)
NOUN: Strong belief in something or someone such as oneself.

consequential
(*kon-si-KWEN-shuhl*)
ADJECTIVE: Significant; having consequence.

contemptuous

(*kuhn-TEMP-choo-uhs*)

NOUN: Feeling disdain or scorn. A *contemptuous* act is one that flies in the face of established procedures or traditions.

contemptuousness

(*kuhn-TEMP-choo-uhs-nes*)

NOUN: To act with disdain or scorn.

content

(*kon-TENT*)

NOUN: Satisfied.

> *After being made to sit out for missing practice, the team's star athlete sat on the bench with a smug look of CONTENT as he watched his team lose.*

contumelious

(*KON-too-muh-lee-uhs*)

NOUN: Being scornfully arrogant toward someone or something in language, action, or treatment.

contumely

(*KON-too-muh-lee*)

NOUN: A rude display in speech or deed; contemptuous behavior. *Contumely* can also mean humiliating derision.

He that is proud eats up himself. Pride is his own glass, his own trumpet, his own chronicle; and whatever praises itself but in the deed, devours the deed in the praise.

—WILLIAM SHAKESPEARE

conviction

(*kuhn-VIK-shuhn*)

NOUN: Firmly held belief in someone or something.

cornstarchy airs

(*KAWRN-stahrch-ee airz*)

PHRASE: An arrogant or haughty attitude.

> *Katherine needs to learn that, as a newcomer, her CORNSTARCHY AIRS won't work in an office full of men and women that have been doing this for thirty years.*

courtliness

(*KAWRT-lee-nes*)

NOUN: Insincerely flattering.

coxcomb

(*KOKS-kohm*)

NOUN: A dandy, conceited man.

coxcombical

(*koks-KOHM-ih-kuhl*)

ADJECTIVE: To do something in a conceited way.

cream of the crop

(*kreem ov thuh krop*)

PHRASE: The best amongst a group.

crow

(*kroh*)

VERB: To speak in a gloating or boastful way.
Derived from the noise a cock makes.

cynical

(*SIN-ih-kuhl*)

ADJECTIVE: The cynics were a group of ancient
Greek philosophers who rejected all conventions
and conventional behavior. In modern times, a *cynical* person is one who thinks the worst of human
nature, often in a smug and self-superior way.

D

damnedest
(*DAM-dist*)
ADJECTIVE: Utmost; best efforts.

dapper
(*DAP-er*)
ADJECTIVE: Very stylishly and neatly dressed.

dauntless
(*DAWNT-lis*)
ADJECTIVE: Unable to be intimidated or put down;
brave; fearless.

debonair
(*deb-uh-NAYR*)
ADJECTIVE: Possessing a polished charm; suave.

deify
(*DEE-uh-fy*)
VERB: To elevate to the level of divinity. When
something is deified, it is exalted or revered as
godlike.

> *Marcus expects any woman he dates to DEIFY him
> and practically worship the ground he walks on.*

A confessional passage has probably never been written that didn't stink a little bit of the writer's pride in having given up his pride.

—J. D. SALINGER

deign
(*dayn*)
VERB: To do something that is below oneself, sometimes in a condescending manner.

dictatorial
(*dik-tuh-TAWR-ee-uhl*)
ADJECTIVE: Bossy.

dignity
(*DIG-ni-tee*)
NOUN: Being worthy of respect or praise.

disdain
(*dis-DAYN*)
NOUN: To treat with contempt; to dismiss haughtily. To *disdain* is to reject due to unworthiness.

disdainfully
(*dis-DAYN-fuhl-ee*)
ADVERB: To do or say something with contempt.

disparity
(*dih-SPAYR-ih-tee*)
NOUN: The condition of being inequivalent or unequal. *Disparity* is inequality in age, measure, or extent.

distinction

(*dih-STINGK-shuhn*)

NOUN: Superiority, excellence.

> *After earning his doctorate, Neil refused to respond to anyone who spoke to him unless they acknowledged his DISTINCTION by addressing him as Dr. Williams.*

domain

(*doh-MAYN*)

NOUN: The territory over which one rules or claims stake to.

domineering

(*dom-uh-NEER-ing*)

ADJECTIVE: Arrogantly overbearing.

draw the long bow

(*draw thuh lawng boh*)

PHRASE: Euphemism for boasting or exaggerating.

driven

(*DRIV-uhn*)

ADJECTIVE: Determined to excel.

E

eclipse
(*ih-KLIPS*)
VERB: To overshadow.

effrontery
(*ih-FRUHN-tuh-ree*)
NOUN: Impudent boldness. *Effrontery* is shameless audacity.

egghead
(*EG-hed*)
NOUN: An intellectual.

ego
(*EE-goh*)
NOUN: A psychological term for the space between the conscious and unconscious, ego has come to mean self-esteem or self-image.

ego trip
(*EE-go trip*)
NOUN: An act done out of self-interest.

ego-tripper
(*EE-go-trip-er*)
NOUN: A person who often goes on ego trips.

egocentric

(*ee-goh-SEN-trik*)

ADJECTIVE: Selfish; tending toward the belief that one's own existence is all-important. An *egocentric* person places his interests above those of all others.

egocentricity

(*ee-goh-sen-TRIS-ih-tee*)

NOUN: A selfish, egocentric attitude.

David's overwhelming EGOCENTRICITY stemmed from the fact his parents always told him he was the best at whatever he did—and now he expects everyone in his adult life to do the same.

egoism

(*EE-goh-iz-uhm*)

NOUN: Valuing things only in reference to one's own self-worth.

egomania

(*ee-goh-MAY-nee-uh*)

NOUN: Obsessive egoism.

egomaniac

(*ee-goh-MAY-nee-ak*)

NOUN: A person who exhibits egomania.

egosurfing
(*ee-goh-SUR-fing*)
NOUN: A slang term meaning to look yourself up on the Internet for the sake of vanity.

egotism
(*EE-guh-tiz-uhm*)
NOUN: Another term for egoism; denotes arrogance and boastfulness.

egotistical
(*ee-guh-TIS-ti-kuhl*)
ADJECTIVE: Selfish and given to vanity; pertaining to egotism.

egotize
(*EE-goh-tyz*)
VERB: To refer to oneself.

eidolon
(*aye-DOH-luhn*)
NOUN: Someone who is so good at something that they deserve imitation.

elder
(*EL-der*)
ADJECTIVE: Of higher rank; superior.

elegant

(*EL-ih-guhnt*)

ADJECTIVE: Having a refined style, taste, and poise.

elite

(*ih-LEET*)

NOUN: The best group of people in a particular category.

elitism

(*ih-LEE-tiz-uhm*)

NOUN: Adherence to the belief that leadership is best managed by an elite (a group considered to be the highest or best class). *Elitism* often carries negative overtones of snobbery.

The ELITISM exuded by the society ladies during their luncheons thoroughly intimidates the waitstaff to the point where they fear speaking.

emblazon

(*em-BLAY-zuhn*)

VERB: To praise or celebrate a person; glorify.

Pride that dines on vanity,

sups on contempt.

—Benjamin Franklin

eminence

(*EM-uh-nuhns*)

NOUN: Superiority or outstanding notability. An eminent person is one of great achievements or high rank. *Eminence* may be used as part of a formal form of address.

eminent

(*EM-uh-nuhnt*)

ADJECTIVE: Prominent or noted; of high esteem; outstanding and distinguished.

empty pride

(*EMP-tee pryd*)

NOUN: Pride with no basis.

ennoble

(*en-NOH-buhl*)

VERB: To elevate or confer dignity upon someone or something.

espouse

(*ih-SPOUZ*)

VERB: To advocate as though one's own. *Espouse* can also mean to take in marriage.

esteem

(*ih-STEEM*)

VERB: To hold in high regard.

ethnocentrism

(*eth-noh-SEN-triz-uhm*)

NOUN: Excessive pride in one's ethnicity to the point where one feels superior to all other ethnicities.

exaggerate

(*ig-ZAJ-uh-rayt*)

VERB: Making something seem larger or greater than it really is.

Even though his feats on the open ocean were already quite remarkable, the sea captain did not hesitate to EXAGGERATE his adventures even more so.

exalt

(*ig-ZAWLT*)

VERB: Glorify or praise; hold up high in honor.

exalted

(*ig-ZAWL-tid*)

NOUN: Filled with pride.

excessive

(*ik-SES-iv*)

ADJECTIVE: More than necessary.

exemplar

(*ig-ZEM-plahr*)

NOUN: The original, to which all future examples are compared.

exhibitionism

(*ek-suh-BISH-uh-niz-uhm*)

NOUN: Acting in such a way as to purposefully draw attention to oneself. Also, the act of displaying one's genitals in public.

extol

(*ik-STOHL*)

VERB: To praise highly.

> *After being showered with praise for his debut concert, the young pianist expects critics to EXTOL every concert he plays, even if they are nowhere near the caliber of his first outing.*

exult

(*ig-ZUHLT*)

VERB: To celebrate or rejoice heartily.

F

fastuous

(*FAS-choo-uhs*)

ADJECTIVE: Haughty and arrogant.

> *Despite her beauty, Mariah remained a social pariah due to her FASTUOUS behavior.*

fish for compliments

(*fish fawr KOM-pluh-mentz*)

VERB: To attempt to get someone to pay a compliment.

flag-waving

(*flag-WAY-ving*)

ADJECTIVE: Intensely patriotic or chauvinistic.

flaunt

(*flawnt*)

VERB: To display (oneself or a possession) in an ostentatious way. *Flaunt* is often confused with flout, but the words have completely different meanings.

flauntingly

(*FLAWN-ting-lee*)

ADVERB: To do or say something in a flaunting, ostentatious way.

The infinitely little have

pride infinitely great.

—Voltaire

flush
(*fluhsh*)
NOUN: Wealthy or having a lot of something like money.

foofaraw
(*FOO-fuh-raw*)
NOUN: A lot of fuss about a lot of nothing, or an excessive amount of decoration on oneself, in a room, etc.

fop
(*fop*)
NOUN: A dandy. An extravagant (male) person who is uncommonly vain or pretentious is a *fop*.

foppish
(*FOP-ish*)
ADJECTIVE: A person concerned with appearance in a pretentious way.

forward
(*FAWR-werd*)
ADJECTIVE: Presumptuous, bold.

fulfilled
(*fuhl-FILD*)
NOUN: A sense of satisfaction or happiness.

fustian

(*FUHS-chuhn*)

NOUN: Pompous, inflated language in writing or speech.

The FUSTIAN memoir was full of intimate, overblown details of the author's life that no one really wanted to know.

G

garland
(*GAHR-luhnd*)
NOUN: A wreath given as an award; an accolade.

gasbag
(*GAS-bag*)
NOUN: A slang term for someone who talks too much about themselves.

> *Even in his old age, the billionaire tycoon was quite the GASBAG, always going on and on about the fortune he amassed over the years.*

gasconade
(*gas-kuh-NAYD*)
NOUN: Boastful talk.

gentry
(*JEN-tree*)
NOUN: People of an upper or ruling class.

gifted
(*GIF-tid*)
ADJECTIVE: Possessing a natural-born talent.

give oneself airs
(*giv wuhn-self airz*)
PHRASE: To act in a haughty way.

When dealing with people,

let us remember we are

not dealing with creatures

of logic. We are dealing

with creatures of emotion,

creatures bustling with

prejudices and motivated by

pride and vanity.

—DALE CARNEGIE

glorify

(*GLAWR-uh-fy*)

VERB: To make something or someone seem better than it actually is.

glory in

(*GLAWR-ee in*)

VERB: To take pleasure or pride in something.

godsend

(*GOD-send*)

NOUN: A helpful person or event that comes unexpectedly.

"Your GODSEND has arrived," Jonathan haughtily announced as he swept into the room, fully believing everyone was waiting on him.

golden

(*GOHL-dun*)

ADJECTIVE: Assured success.

grandeur

(*GRAN-jer*)

NOUN: The quality of being grand; extravagance in scale or appearance. *Grandeur* refers to magnificence.

grandiloquence

(*gran-DIL-uh-kwuhns*)

NOUN: Pompous speech or expression; bombast. *Grandiloquence* refers to an attitude of haughtiness, especially in one's means of communication.

grandiose

(*GRAN-dee-ohs*)

ADJECTIVE: Pompous. Someone whose pretentions or ambitions exceed his abilities, sensitivities, or means could be considered *grandiose*.

gravitas

(*GRAV-ih-tahs*)

NOUN: Importance.

H

hail
(*hayl*)
VERB: To praise and applaud passionately.

haughty
(*HAW-tee*)
ADJECTIVE: Snobbishly proud.

haughty airs
(*HAW-tee airz*)
PHRASE: A haughty and snobbish attitude.

hauteur
(*hoh-TUR*)
NOUN: Haughty in manner.

have a big head
(*hav uh big hed*)
VERB: To think very highly of oneself, often without merit.

heavy hitter
(*HEV-ee HIT-ter*)
NOUN: A very important and powerful person.

herald
(*HAIR-uhld*)
VERB: To proclaim or make known.

Pride goeth before

destruction, and an haughty

spirit before a fall.

—Proverbs 16:18

hero

(*HEER-oh*)

NOUN: A person who is recognized for his remarkable bravery and great courage.

heroic

(*he-ROH-ik*)

ADJECTIVE: Possessing the attributes of a hero; brave.

high and mighty

(*hy and my-tee*)

ADJECTIVE: An informal way of referring to someone who acts more important than everyone else.

> *Thalia looked at her husband arguing with the server over the taste of the champagne and wondered how his HIGH AND MIGHTY attitude had developed without her noticing.*

high hat

(*HY hat*)

ADJECTIVE: Snobbish and haughty.

high horse

(*HY hawrs*)

NOUN: Someone who is displaying arrogant qualities is said to be on his or her *high horse*.

highbrow

(*HY-brou*)

ADJECTIVE: Intelligent and cultured; also, one who is pretentious or snobby about intelligence and culture.

highfalutin

(*hy-fuh-LOOT-n*)

ADJECTIVE: Pompous; pretentious; overblown and extravagant.

high-flown

(*HY-flohn*)

ADJECTIVE: Pretentious and lofty.

highflying

(*HY-FLY-ing*)

ADJECTIVE: Lofty in an unduly way.

high-nosed

(*HY-nohz-duh*)

ADJECTIVE: Stuck up, proud. A person who looks down on someone or something.

high-toned

(*HY-tohnd*)

ADJECTIVE: Superior in a stylish way.

his or her nibs

(*hiz awr hur nibz*)

NOUN: When an authoritative figure is demanding to the point of tyranny. Another way of saying "his or her majesty," in a facetious manner.

hoity-toity

(*HOY-tee-TOY-tee*)

ADJECTIVE: Pretentious; haughty; snobbish.

> "I only book rooms in five-star establishments," the HOITY-TOITY woman said to the concierge. "If I'm unhappy with the accommodations, I'll be leaving immediately."

hold one's head high

(*hohld wuhnz hed hy*)

PHRASE: This idiom means to behave proudly.

hold up one's head

(*hohld up wuhnz hed*)

PHRASE: See *hold one's head high.*

holier-than-thou

(*HOH-lee-er-thuhn-thow*)

ADJECTIVE: An attitude of moral superiority.

hot-dog

(*HOT-dawg*)

VERB: To show off in front of a group of people, usually by doing something dangerous.

hubris

(*HYOO-bris*)

NOUN: Excessive pride. *Hubris* can refer to the "fatal flaw" of ancient Greek drama or (more generally) to any disproportionate pride or self-love.

> *Many of literature's greatest heroes became undone by their HUBRIS, allowing their own pride to be their worst enemy.*

hubristic

(*HYOO-bris-tik*)

ADJECTIVE: Displaying excessive pride.

huff

(*huhf*)

VERB: An obsolete term meaning to treat someone arrogantly. This can also mean to swell with pride.

hype

(*hyp*)

VERB: To garner attention using over-the-top tactics.

I

⫘

immodest

(*ih-MOD-ist*)

NOUN: Lacking in humility, showing an exaggerated sense of self-worth.

immodestly

(*ih-MOD-ist-lee*)

ADVERB: To act in a bold way that shows a lack of decency.

imperious

(*im-PEER-ee-uhs*)

ADJECTIVE: Haughty. Also: urgent. *Imperious* is usually meant to convey a sense of dictatorial arrogance.

impertinence

(*im-PUR-tn-uhns*)

NOUN: The action of being impertinent.

> *The young man's IMPERTINENCE was invisible to no one but himself; his treatment of the bank teller defined disrespectful.*

impertinent

(*im-PUR-tn-uhnt*)

ADJECTIVE: Rude; brash. Something that is improper or beyond established bounds is *impertinent*.

importunate

(*im-PAWR-chuh-nit*)

ADJECTIVE: Demanding or impatient in issuing repeated requests. An *importunate* person makes many annoying entreaties.

importune

(*im-pawr-TOON*)

VERB: To request repeatedly so as to be a bother.

impudent

(*IM-pyuh-duhnt*)

NOUN: Not showing respect.

independence

(*in-di-PEN-duhns*)

NOUN: The state of being not reliant on anyone else.

independent

(*in-di-PEN-duhnt*)

ADJECTIVE: Self-reliant and not dependent on anyone else for livelihood or subsistence.

A proud man is always

looking down on things and

people; and, of course, as

long as you're looking down,

you can't see something

that's above you.

—C. S. LEWIS

inflated

(*in-FLAY-tid*)

NOUN: Puffed up, full of air. Someone who is arrogant might be said to have an inflated ego.

insolence

(*IN-suh-luhns*)

NOUN: The act of being rude and arrogant.

insolent

(*IN-suh-luhnt*)

ADJECTIVE: Rude and arrogant. That which is insulting or disrespectful (especially speech) could be considered *insolent*.

> *The hostess' INSOLENT retorts to Joan's well-intentioned queries stunned the dinner party.*

introspection

(*in-truh-SPEK-shuhn*)

NOUN: Self-examination; interior meditation. To think closely on one's feelings, thoughts, and inclinations is to spend time in *introspection*.

J and K

jack-a-dandy

(*jak-uh-DAN-dee*)

NOUN: An impertinent, conceited young man.

jackanapes

(*JAK-uh-nayps*)

NOUN: An arrogant or impertinent person; especially an impudent young man.

> *Walter realized what a JACKANAPES his grandson had become after asking him about his future goals.*

jactation

(*jak-TAY-shuhn*)

NOUN: A rare way of saying boasting or bragging (tossing words about), this also means restlessly tossing the body.

jerk

(*jurk*)

NOUN: A rude person.

jumped-up

(*JUHMPT-uhp*)

ADJECTIVE: Rising in significance in an arrogant way.

He who does not need to lie

is proud of not being a liar.

—FRIEDRICH NIETZSCHE

keen

(*keen*)

ADJECTIVE: Characterized by a mental sharpness or heightened sense.

key

(*kee*)

ADJECTIVE: Fundamental; of the utmost importance.

knockout

(*NOK-out*)

NOUN: A person who is exceedingly beautiful or overwhelmingly remarkable.

know-all

(*NOH-awl*)

NOUN: Someone who comes across as being knowledgeable.

know-it-all

(*NOH-it-awl*)

NOUN: A person who acts as if he or she knows everything about anything.

kvell

(*kvel*)

VERB: A Yiddish word meaning to be extremely proud.

L

lambaste
(*lam-BAYST*)
VERB: To criticize in a harsh and condescending manner; berate.

larrikin
(*LAR-ih-kin*)
NOUN/ADJECTIVE: Of Australian origin, meaning a boisterous, arrogant young man.

laudable
(*LAW-duh-buhl*)
ADJECTIVE: Worthy or deserving of praise.

lead
(*leed*)
VERB: To take charge; to go first.

leader
(*LEE-der*)
NOUN: One who takes control of a situation and acts a guide.

legendary
(*LEJ-uhn-der-ee*)
ADJECTIVE: Impressive enough to be retold; extremely well known.

lineage

(*LIN-ee-ij*)

NOUN: The line of descent from an ancestor; pedigree.

loftiness

(*LAWF-tee-nes*)

NOUN: To act in a lofty way.

lofty

(*LAWF-tee*)

ADJECTIVE: Aloof; pretentious; arrogant in a superior way.

lofty-minded

(*LAWF-tee-myn-did*)

ADJECTIVE: Characterized by elevated, often arrogant, ideals.

look big

(*look big*)

PHRASE: An expression meaning to walk pompously as if showing off; to walk with swagger.

look one in the face or eye

(*look wuhn in thuh fays awr aye*)

PHRASE: An expression meaning to be too proud to back down.

lordly airs

(*LAWRD-lee airz*)

NOUN: Having an attitude implying that one is better than others; acting in a pretentious or lordly, regal way.

The LORDLY AIRS Jeffery exuded after returning from Europe were not kindly received by his family.

M

machismo
(*mah-CHEEZ-moh*)
NOUN: From the Spanish word for male, meaning aggressive masculine pride.

macho
(*MAH-choh*)
ADJECTIVE: Excessive, masculine pride.

magisterial
(*maj-uh-STEER-ee-uhl*)
ADJECTIVE: Dictatorial; done with an air of authority.

> *The charity's board was supposed to make decisions as a group, but one of the members took a MAGISTERIAL position and began making decisions without consulting her fellow members.*

magniloquent
(*mag-NIL-uh-kwuhnt*)
ADJECTIVE: Using bombastic language to impress.

majesty
(*MAJ-uh-stee*)
ADJECTIVE: Greatness, stateliness, dignity.

Vanity and pride are
different things, though
the words are often used
synonymously. A person may
be proud without being vain.
Pride relates more to our
opinion of ourselves; vanity,
to what we would have
others think of us.

—JANE AUSTEN

malapert

(*MAL-uh-purt*)

ADJECTIVE: Impudently bold and disrespectful.

masturbatory

(*MAS-ter-buh-tawr-ee*)

ADJECTIVE: Relating to self-satisfaction. Technically this term means relating to masturbation or physically bringing oneself to orgasm.

megalomania

(*meg-uh-loh-MAY-nee-uh*)

NOUN: Delusions of wealth and/or power. Literally, *megalomania* is a psychopathological condition in which a person is obsessed with fantasies of riches or authority. The word is also used to describe people whose ambitions and sense of self-importance are overblown.

> *Some interpreted the actor's purchase of an old castle as an uncharacteristically bad real estate deal; I see it as pure MEGALOMANIA.*

miserly

(*MY-zer-lee*)

ADJECTIVE: Characteristic of a person who hoards wealth.

Many a man is praised for

his reserve and so-called

shyness when he is simply

too proud to risk making a

fool of himself.

—J. B. PRIESTLEY

N

narcissism

(*NAHR-suh-siz-em*)

NOUN: Excessive self-interest or self-love.

narcissist

(*NAHR-suh-sizt*)

NOUN: A person who exhibits excessive self-interest or self-love.

narcissistic

(*nahr-suh-SIZ-tik*)

ADJECTIVE: Possessed by self-love. Someone whose egotism replaces (or seems to replace) attention to others can be said to be *narcissistic*.

> *Trying to get ahead is one thing; the NARCISSISTIC zeal with which Gerald speaks about himself is quite another.*

narcissistic personality disorder (NPD)

(*nahr-suh-SIZ-tik pur-suh-NAL-ih-tee dis-AWR-der*)

NOUN: A psychological condition in which someone has a disproportionate self-preoccupation as well as an inflated sense of self-importance.

Narcissus

(*nahr-SIS-uhs*)

NOUN: In Greek mythology, a young man who fell in love with his own reflection in a pool of water.

The intelligent man who is

proud of his intelligence is

like the condemned man

who is proud of his large cell.

—Simone Weil

neat

(*neet*)

ADJECTIVE: Well put together; properly groomed.

noble

(*NOH-bul*)

ADJECTIVE: Showing qualities of or relating to a high social class.

notability

(*noh-tuh-BIL-ih-tee*)

NOUN: The state or quality of being worthy of recognition.

notable

(*NOH-tuh-buhl*)

ADJECTIVE: Worthy of being noticed; prominent.

notorious

(*noh-TOHR-ee-us*)

ADJECTIVE: Very well known, but typically not for a good reason.

number one

(*NUHM-ber wuhn*)

ADJECTIVE: First-rate; the best.

O

obstinate

(*OB-stuh-nit*)

ADJECTIVE: Unyielding. Someone who holds firmly to an opinion, attitude, or approach despite obstacles could be said to be *obstinate*.

obtrusive

(*uhb-TROO-siv*)

ADJECTIVE: Behavior that is self-assertive and forward.

offish

(*AW-fish*)

ADJECTIVE: Aloof and unfriendly; pretentious.

Olympian loftiness or detachment

(*uh-LIM-pee-uhn LAWF-tee-nes awr dih-TACH-muhnt*)

NOUN: Someone who feels themselves superior to others and mundane matters.

> *With a sense of OLYMPIAN DETACHMENT, he told us that he could not attend the dinner party that weekend because he would be traversing the Alps during a private ski vacation.*

optimal

(*OP-tuh-muhl*)

ADJECTIVE: The best of something or the most favorable.

God opposes the proud,

but gives grace to the

humble [James 4:6].

—BIBLE

orgulous

(*AWR-gyuh-luhs*)

ADJECTIVE: Derived from the French word *orguill* meaning "pride," this is a literary term meaning haughty.

orotund

(*AWR-uh-tuhnd*)

ADJECTIVE: Pompous style, expression, speech, or writing.

ostentation

(*os-ten-TAY-shuhn*)

NOUN: A boastful, vulgar display.

> *The homes of the nouveau riche typically reek of OSTENTATION as they try to make their newfound wealth as obvious as possible.*

ostentatious

(*os-ten-TAY-shuhs*)

ADJECTIVE: Showy. Someone who makes a boastful display, or makes constant attempts to show off talents or possessions, could be said to be *ostentatious*.

outrecuidance

(*oo-tre-KWEE-dens*)

NOUN: Excessive presumption.

overbearing
(*oh-ver-BAYR-ing*)
ADJECTIVE: Arrogantly dominant.

overblown
(*oh-ver-BLOHN*)
ADJECTIVE: Pretentious; excessively inflated attitude.

overconfident
(*oh-ver-KON-fi-duhnt*)
ADJECTIVE: Excessively confident.

overproud
(*oh-ver-PROUD*)
NOUN: Excessively proud.

overweeningly
(*oh-ver-WEE-ning-lee*)
ADVERB: In an overconfident, proud way.

overwise
(*oh-ver-WYZ*)
ADJECTIVE: Excessively, affectedly wise.

P

panegyric
(*pan-ih-JIR-ik*)
NOUN: Formal, elaborate praise.

paramount
(*PAR-uh-mount*)
ADJECTIVE: More important or supreme than others; above others in rank and authority.

pardonable pride
(*PAHR-duhn-uh-buhl pryd*)
PHRASE: Pride that is excusable.

patronize
(*PAY-truh-nyz*)
VERB: This word can mean simply to give a business your patronage, but *patronize* usually has a negative meaning, suggesting that one is being condescending toward another.

pay one's own way
(*pey wuhnz ohn way*)
PHRASE: A phrase meaning independent; too proud to ask for help.

peacock
(*PEE-kok*)
NOUN: A vain, showy person.

peacockish
(*PEE-kok-ish*)
ADJECTIVE: To display oneself in a vain or showy way.

pedant
(*PED-nt*)
NOUN: A person who displays learning inappropriately or excessively; also, someone who focuses too narrowly on rules and minor details.

> *Do not get Roland started on Shakespearean tragedy; he's a shameless PEDANT who'll dominate an entire discussion with observations on the time problem in* Othello.

peremptory
(*puh-REMP-tuh-ree*)
ADJECTIVE: Assertive and imperious, requiring immediate attention.

perk
(*purk*)
VERB: To hold up the head or body in a bold or insolent manner.

pert
(*purt*)
ADJECTIVE: Bold and impudent, in speech or behavior.

We are rarely proud

when we are alone.

—VOLTAIRE

pique (oneself)
(*peek wuhn-self*)
VERB: An archaic way of saying pride oneself.

pomp
(*pomp*)
NOUN: A dignified ceremony, or an archaic way of saying boastful or ostentatious display.

> *The executor clearly enjoyed his moment in the sun, reading the will with more POMP than many thought it warranted.*

pomp and circumstance
(*pomp and SUR-kuhm-stans*)
NOUN: Ceremony and fuss. Also the name of the popular song played at graduation and other ceremonies.

pomposity
(*pom-POS-ih-tee*)
NOUN: To do something in a pompous way or with pompous airs.

pompous
(*POM-puhs*)
ADJECTIVE: Pretentious; overblown; self-important.

pompous twit
(*POM-puhs twit*)
NOUN: A derogatory way of saying that someone is not only annoying and pompous but also a nerd or twerp.

pontifical
(*pon-TIF-ih-kuhl*)
ADJECTIVE: Pompous, pretentious air.

popinjay
(*POP-in-jay*)
NOUN: Derived from the Spanish word for parrot, this term has come to mean a vainly talkative person or someone who likes to talk in order to hear the sound of his or her own voice.

positive self-image
(*POZ-ih-tiv self-IM-ij*)
NOUN: A healthy dose of pride.

praise
(*prayz*)
VERB: Express approval or admiration of someone or something.

preen
(*preen*)
VERB: To primp; to perfect one's appearance. Also: to take pride in oneself or one's accomplishments.

preen oneself
(*preen wuhn-SELF*)
VERB: To take pride in one's accomplishments.

preoccupied with oneself
(*pree-OK-yuh-pyd with wuhn-SELF*)
PHRASE: Being engrossed in one's own affairs.

> *Benjamin didn't notice how hurt the girl looked when he walked past without acknowledging her existence; he was too PREOCCUPIED WITH HIMSELF.*

presumption
(*pri-ZUHMP-shuhn*)
NOUN: Impertinent boldness; unwarranted assumption.

presumptuous
(*pri-ZUHMP-choo-uhs*)
NOUN: Bold behavior, without necessarily realizing that it is not appropriate.

pretentious

(*pri-TEN-shuhs*)

ADJECTIVE: An assumption of importance; ostentatious.

> *The PRETENTIOUS professor would take any opportunity he could to speak down to his students and redirect any discussion back to his own body of work.*

pride

(*pryd*)

NOUN: This word has several meanings, including a group of lions and LGBTQ pride (as in a Pride Parade). Most importantly though, it means a deep feeling of pleasure or satisfaction taken from either one's own achievements or the achievements of those with whom one associates.

pride goes (or comes) before a fall

(*pryd gohz [awr kuhmz] bih-FAWR uh fawl*)

PHRASE: Something bad happening to someone because he or she was too conceited.

pride of place

(*pryd ov plays*)

PHRASE: The highest position.

If a man is proud of his

wealth, he should not be

praised until it is known

how he employs it.

—SOCRATES

pridefully

(*PRYD-fool-ee*)

ADVERB: To act with satisfaction taken from one's own achievements.

prig

(*prig*)

NOUN: A person who acts morally superior to others. See *self-righteous*.

prima donna

(*pree-muh DON-uh*)

NOUN: A self-centered member of a group or organization who feels that his contributions are so important as to merit special treatment. (Literally, a *prima donna* is the leading female singer in an opera company.)

proud

(*prowd*)

NOUN: Excessively pleased or satisfied with one's own accomplishments or with the accomplishments of those with whom one is closely associated with. This can be seen in a positive light or an extremely negative light (as in the sin of pride).

proud as a peacock

(*prowd az uh PEE-kok*)

PHRASE: A person who is excessively proud.

Linda was PROUD AS A PEACOCK when a wing of the library was dedicated in her family's name.

proud as Lucifer

(*prowd az LOO-suh-fer*)

PHRASE: A proverbial phrase meaning haughty and arrogant. Derived from the fact that Satan was called Lucifer and was expelled from heaven for being too prideful.

proud as punch

(*prowd az puhnch*)

PHRASE: An idiom originating from the main character of the Punch and Judy show, meaning that someone is acting with displayable pride.

proud-blooded

(*prowd-BLUHD-id*)

ADJECTIVE: Used to describe someone who has pride running through his or her veins or was clearly born to a proud family.

proudhearted

(*PROWD-hahr-tid*)

ADJECTIVE: Arrogant; haughty.

proud-looking

(*prowd-LOO-king*)

ADJECTIVE: Used to describe someone who is clearly pleased with something that he or she has done or accomplished.

proud-minded

(*prowd-MYN-did*)

ADJECTIVE: Used to describe someone who is too proud to do something that is apparently below him or her. Most notably used in Shakespeare's *Taming of the Shrew* to describe Katherine, who is sharp-tongued and quick-tempered.

proud-spirited

(*prowd-SPIR-i-tid*)

ADJECTIVE: Another way of saying proud-blooded.

puffed-up

(*PUHFT-uhp*)

ADJECTIVE: Literally swollen or full of air, but also self-important and pompous.

pull rank

(*puhl rangk*)

VERB: Asserting or taking advantage of seniority.

> *Always one to PULL RANK, the company's division
> president had no qualms about arriving late to the
> presentation and requesting a junior staff member give
> him his seat.*

puppy

(*PUHP-ee*)

NOUN: A derogatory term for a young man who is
brash, conceited, or arrogant.

purse-pride

(*PURS-pryd*)

NOUN: Pride derived from the amount of money
that one has; arrogance related to one's wealth.

pursy

(*PUR-see*)

ADJECTIVE: Another way of saying purse-pride or
arrogantly rich.

R

regality

(*ri-GAL-ih-tee*)

NOUN: The demeanor of royalty or privilege.

reputation

(*rep-yuh-TAY-shuhn*)

NOUN: Beliefs or estimations held about someone or something.

Even though the artist's REPUTATION preceded him, the gallery owner was still taken aback by how haughty and demeaning he was during their conversation.

righteous

(*RY-chuhs*)

ADJECTIVE: Morally right; justifiable; virtuous.

rodomontade

(*rod-uh-mon-TAYD*)

NOUN: Boastful talk or behavior.

roister

(*ROY-ster*)

VERB: To celebrate loudly or in a boastful way.

I will give you a definition

of a proud man: he is a man

who has neither vanity nor

wisdom—one filled with

hatreds cannot be vain,

neither can he be wise.

—JOHN KEATS

S

sangfroid
(*sahn-FRWAH*)
NOUN: The state of being supremely composed or self-assured, especially in the face of adversity or danger.

satisfaction
(*sat-is-FAK-shuhn*)
NOUN: Pleasure derived from the fulfillment of expectations.

satisfy
(*SAT-is-fy*)
VERB: To meet needs or desires.

saucebox
(*SAWS-boks*)
NOUN: An impudent person.

self
(*self*)
NOUN: A person's essential being, identity, character, abilities, and attitudes, especially in relation to people or things outside oneself.

self-absorbed

(*SELF-ab-SAWRBD*)

ADJECTIVE: Preoccupied by one's own thoughts, emotions, and situation in life.

William was too SELF-ABSORBED to notice that everyone rolled their eyes every time he started to speak.

self-absorption

(*SELF-ab-SAWRP-shuhn*)

NOUN: Preoccupation with one's own thoughts, emotions, and situation in life.

self-admiration

(*SELF-ad-muh-RAY-shuhn*)

NOUN: The adoring of oneself.

self-adulation

(*SELF-ad-uh-LAY-shuhn*)

NOUN: Self-flattery.

self-advertisement

(*SELF-ad-ver-TYZ-muhnt*)

NOUN: Actively publicizing one's own self.

self-advocacy

(*SELF-AD-vuh-kuh-see*)

NOUN: Standing up for one's own beliefs or interests.

self-aggrandizement

(*SELF-uh-GRAN-dyz-ment*)

NOUN: Advancing one's place in life or increasing one's power, often through aggressive means.

The politician would never deny that he was guilty of SELF-AGGRANDIZEMENT during the campaign season.

self-applauding

(*SELF-uh-PLAW-ding*)

ADJECTIVE: An excessive feeling of pride or approval in oneself.

self-approval

(*SELF-uh-PROO-vuhl*)

NOUN: Approval of oneself.

self-asserting

(*SELF-uh-SUR-ting*)

ADJECTIVE: Confident self-advertisement.

self-assurance
(*SELF-uh-SHOOR-uhns*)
NOUN: Confidence in one's abilities.

self-awareness
(*SELF-uh-WAIR-nes*)
NOUN: Knowledge of the self or of one's character or personality.

self-centered
(*SELF-SEN-terd*)
ADJECTIVE: Vain, concerned only with one's own needs and desires.

self-centeredness
(*SELF-SEN-terd-nes*)
NOUN: The act of being concerned with one's own needs, desires, and affairs.

self-conceit
(*SELF-kuhn-SEET*)
NOUN: An excessive view of one's abilities or qualities.

self-confidence
(*SELF-KON-fi-duhns*)
NOUN: Trust in one's own abilities.

self-congratulation

(*SELF-kuhn-graj-uh-LAY-shuhn*)

NOUN: Complacent acknowledgement or pride regarding one's own achievements or qualities. Self-satisfaction.

self-delight

(*SELF-dih-LYT*)

NOUN: Pleasure in oneself.

self-display

(*SELF-dih-SPLAY*)

NOUN: To put oneself on display.

self-esteem

(*SELF-ih-STEEM*)

NOUN: Confidence in oneself; satisfaction with one's own worth.

self-exaltation

(*SELF-eg-zawl-TAY-shuhn*)

NOUN: Holding oneself in high regard.

self-flattering

(*SELF-FLAT-ter-ing*)

ADJECTIVE: Given to holding a high opinion of oneself.

A proud man is seldom a

grateful man, for he never

thinks he gets as much as he

deserves.

—HENRY WARD BEECHER

self-flattery

(*SELF-FLAT-ter-ee*)

NOUN: Focusing on one's good qualities and holding a high opinion of oneself because of those qualities (while disregarding any weaknesses).

self-glorification

(*SELF-glawr-uh-fi-KAY-shuhn*)

NOUN: Bragging about one's abilities or expressing superiority.

self-gratification

(*SELF-grat-uh-fi-KAY-shuhn*)

NOUN: Satisfying one's desires by pleasing oneself.

After witnessing Patrick's egregious act of SELF-GRATIFCATION, Claire knew that she could no longer stay in a relationship with him.

self-importance

(*SELF-im-PAWR-tns*)

NOUN: An exaggerated estimate of one's own value.

self-indulgence

(*SELF-in-DUHL-juhns*)

NOUN: Gratification of one's own desires.

self-indulgent

(*SELF-in-DUHL-juhnt*)

ADJECTIVE: Doing what one wants, whether or not it is in the best interest of others.

self-interest

(*SELF-IN-trist*)

NOUN: Selfish. Concern for oneself without regard for others.

self-interested

(*SELF-IN-truh-stid*)

ADJECTIVE: Motivated by self-interest.

self-involved

(*SELF-in-VOLVD*)

ADJECTIVE: Absorbed in oneself.

self-love

(*SELF-luhv*)

NOUN: Conceited love for oneself; regard for one's advantage or well-being.

self-opinion

(*SELF-uh-PIN-yuhn*)

NOUN: High opinion of oneself. See *self-conceit*.

self-opinionated

(*SELF-uh-PIN-yuh-nay-tid*)

ADJECTIVE: Conceited; arrogant. Having high regard for oneself.

self-possession

(*SELF-puh-ZESH-uhn*)

NOUN: In control of one's feelings and behavior.

self-praise

(*SELF-prayz*)

NOUN: Boasting; praise of oneself.

While his speech was meant to celebrate the accomplishments of the entire team, Victor took it as an opportunity for SELF-PRAISE, only mentioning what he had done in order to achieve success.

self-regard

(*SELF-ri-GAHRD*)

NOUN: Consideration for oneself in a conceited way.

self-regarding

(*SELF-ri-GAHR-ding*)

ADJECTIVE: Concerned with one's own interests or needs.

self-reliance
(*SELF-ri-LY-uhns*)
NOUN: Dependence on one's own abilities, powers, and resources.

self-reliant
(*SELF-ri-LY-uhnt*)
ADJECTIVE: To act in a way that shows that one is reliant only on oneself.

self-respect
(*SELF-ri-SPEKT*)
NOUN: Confidence in oneself; pride in one's standing or position.

self-righteous
(*SELF-RY-chuhs*)
ADJECTIVE: Convinced that one's own position or opinion is the morally superior, however unfounded that view is.

self-seeking
(*SELF-SEE-king*)
ADJECTIVE: Selfishly advancing one's own agenda.

self-serving
(*SELF-SUR-ving*)
ADJECTIVE: Putting ones own welfare before others.

self-sufficient

(*SELF-suh-FISH-uhnt*)

NOUN: Independent; needing no outside help in order to provide basic needs.

self-validating

(*SELF-VAL-ih-day-ting*)

ADJECTIVE: To remind yourself that you are correct or accurate.

self-valuation

(*SELF-val-yoo-EY-shuhn*)

NOUN: The estimation of one's worth.

self-worship

(*SELF-WUR-ship*)

NOUN: The worship of oneself.

> *While the king had no problem with SELF-WORSHIP—commissioning countless statues and portraits of himself—the people whom he ruled over thought he was a miserable tyrant.*

self-worth

(*SELF-wurth*)

NOUN: See *self-esteem*.

The proud man counts his
newspaper clippings, the
humble man his blessings.

—FULTON J. SHEEN

selfish

(*SEL-fish*)

ADJECTIVE: A person who has his or her own interests at heart and lacks consideration for others.

shoot a line

(*shoot uh lyn*)

PHRASE: An outdated euphemism meaning to boast.

showiness

(*SHOH-ee-nis*)

NOUN: Bright and colorful; ostentatious.

showoff

(*SHOH-awf*)

NOUN: A person who flaunts his or her accomplishments or possessions and publicly preens.

smart-aleck

(*SMAHRT-AL-ik*)

NOUN: Someone who thinks that he or she is clever but in reality is irritating.

smart-ass

(*SMAHRT-as*)

NOUN: A more crass way of saying that someone is a smart-aleck.

smarty
(*SMAHRT-ee*)
NOUN: See *know-it-all*.

smug
(*smuhg*)
ADJECTIVE: Excessive pride in one's achievements.

smugness
(*SMUHG-nes*)
NOUN: Having excessive pride in one's achievements.

sniffy
(*SNIF-ee*)
ADJECTIVE: Disdainful or scornful.

snippy
(*SNIP-ee*)
ADJECTIVE: Haughty or condescending in a sharp, curt way.

snob
(*snob*)
NOUN: A person who looks down on others and feels that his or her beliefs or tastes are superior.

> *Olivia is the epitome of a music SNOB, refusing to attend performances from any ensemble other than the Metropolitan Philharmonic Orchestra.*

snobbish

(*SNOB-ish*)

ADJECTIVE: Characteristic of a snob.

snooty

(*SNOO-tee*)

ADJECTIVE: Showing contempt toward others in an arrogant way.

snotty

(*SNOT-ee*)

ADJECTIVE: An arrogant, snobbish attitude.

soi-disant

(*swa-dee-ZAHN*)

ADJECTIVE: A French term for "oneself saying," meaning self-proclaimed, self-styled.

solipsism

(*SOL-ip-siz-uhm*)

NOUN: The idea that one's own perceptions are the only meaningful reality. *Solipsism* was once used to describe a philosophical doctrine, but it has also been taken to mean the practice of extreme self-centeredness.

solipsistic

(*SOL-ip-siz-tik*)

ADJECTIVE: Acting in a way that implies that one's own perceptions are the only meaningful reality.

The SOLIPSISTIC director was so enraged when his film did not win the festival's top award that he made a scene of storming out of the reception during the winner's acceptance speech.

sonorous

(*suh-NAWR-uhs*)

ADJECTIVE: Deep or rich in sound; also, overblown or conceited in language.

sophomoric

(*sof-MAWR-ik*)

ADJECTIVE: Immature; overbearing in a conceited or pretentious way; characteristic of one with little learning but convinced that he or she is brilliant.

splendiferous

(*splen-DIF-er-uhs*)

ADJECTIVE: Showily impressive.

stand on one's own two feet

(*stand awn wuhnz ohn too feet*)

PHRASE: An idiom meaning independent.

None are more taken in by

flattery than the proud,

who wish to be the first

and are not.

—Baruch Spinoza

stand up straight

(*stand uhp strayt*)

PHRASE: See *hold one's head high.*

standoffish

(*STAND-AW-fish*)

ADJECTIVE: To act uninterested in others due to a feeling or appearance of superiority.

stately

(*STAYT-lee*)

ADJECTIVE: Lofty or majestic in appearance or manner.

> *She walked into the ballroom with a STATELY air, causing the other ladies present to turn, stare, and whisper.*

stiff-necked

(*STIF-NEKT*)

ADJECTIVE: Haughty or arrogant behavior. Someone who is *stiff-necked* is holding his or her head up high due to feelings of superiority.

stroke

(*strohk*)

VERB: Repeatedly brushing, as in to stroke one's ego.

strut

(*struht*)

VERB: To walk with a conceited gait in an arrogant manner.

stubborn

(*STUHB-ern*)

ADJECTIVE: Determination not to change; obstinately unmoving.

> *Unfortunately Jonah thinks he's in the right and is so STUBBORN that no argument could possibly sway him otherwise.*

stuffed shirt

(*stuhfd shurt*)

PHRASE: Similar to being too big for one's own britches, this term means a pompous, often also dull, person.

supercilious

(*soo-per-SIL-ee-uhs*)

ADJECTIVE: Disdainful or haughty. Someone who is overbearingly proud could be said to be supercilious.

superciliousness

(*soo-per-SIL-ee-uhs-nes*)

NOUN: The act of being disdainful or haughty.

superior

(*suh-PEER-ee-er*)

ADJECTIVE: Higher in position, rank, or status than someone or something.

superiority

(*suh-peer-ee-AWR-ih-tee*)

NOUN: The state or condition of being higher in position or rank than someone.

superiority complex

(*suh-peer-ee-AWR-ih-tee KOM-pleks*)

NOUN: Covering up inferiority by putting on an attitude that shows exaggerated superiority.

swagger

(*SWAG-er*)

VERB: To boast or brag, or to walk in an ostentatious way.

swank

(*swangk*)

ADJECTIVE: Fancy or fashionable and pretentious in a showy way. Displaying achievements for others to glory in.

swashbuckling

(*SWOSH-buhk-ling*)

ADJECTIVE: Flamboyant; boastful.

swellheaded

(*SWEL-hed-id*)

ADJECTIVE: A person who is arrogant and bigheaded.

swing the lamp

(*swing thuh lamp*)

PHRASE: A British euphemism meaning to boast.

swollen

(*SWOH-luhn*)

ADJECTIVE: To become larger or more full. Someone with a swollen head or swollen ego would be bigheaded. See *bighead, swellheaded*.

All it took was a compliment from one critic for the chef's ego to become completely SWOLLEN.

T

tact
(*takt*)
NOUN: A sense of what is appropriate or tasteful.

take notice of
(*tayk NOH-tis uhv*)
VERB: To pay attention to.

talent
(*TAL-uhnt*)
NOUN: A special innate ability.

talk down to
(*tawk doun too*)
VERB: To criticize in a demeaning manner.

taste
(*tayst*)
NOUN: The discerning sense of what is excellent in quality.

think no small beer of oneself
(*thingk noh smawl beer ov wuhn-SELF*)
PHRASE: This antiquated expression means to think well of oneself. "Small beer" refers to weak beer.

Fame often makes a writer

vain, but seldom makes

him proud.

—W. H. Auden

thrasonical

(*thray-SON-ih-kuhl*)

ADJECTIVE: Boastful; bragging; vainglorious. This word stems from a braggart of a character named Thraso in Terence's *Eunuchus*.

toffee-nosed

(*TAW-fee-nohzd*)

ADJECTIVE: A British term for someone who thinks themselves smarter or higher-up in society than others.

> *Only someone as TOFFEE-NOSED as Helen would assume the woman tailoring her dress was just a lowly seamstress and not the woman responsible for the clothing's design.*

too big for one's boots

(*too big fawr wuhnz boots*)

PHRASE: Overly confident; having a swollen head or ego.

too big for one's breeches

(*too big fawr wuhnz BRICH-iz*)

PHRASE: Overconfident. This British term comes from the idea of a person being puffed-up or having a swollen ego.

too clever by half

(*too KLEV-er by hahf*)

PHRASE: A condescending way of saying that someone is overly confident in his or her intelligence.

toot one's own horn

(*toot wuhnz ohn hawrn*)

PHRASE: To speak in a prideful way that is focused on one's own accomplishments.

toploftical

(*TOP-LAWF-tee-kal*)

ADJECTIVE: To act in an arrogant or haughty way.

Young Susan began to take on her mother's TOPLOFTICAL attitude when she started barking orders at the maids.

toplofty

(*TOP-LAWF-tee*)

ADJECTIVE: An informal way of saying that someone is arrogant or haughty.

turgid

(*TUR-jid*)

ADJECTIVE: Embellished, pompous language.

turkey cock

(*TUR-kee kok*)

NOUN: A pompous person; one who struts in a conceited manner.

tympany

(*TIM-puh-nee*)

NOUN: An obsolete term meaning arrogant or pretentious, from the medical term *tympanites* meaning an abdomen swollen with air or gas.

U and V

ultimate
(*UHL-tuh-mit*)
ADJECTIVE: Maximum; highest; the best.

unabashed
(*uhn-uh-BASHT*)
ADJECTIVE: Not embarrassed; poised.

unashamed
(*uhn-uh-SHAYMD*)
ADJECTIVE: Not restrained by moral guilt or social norms.

unique
(*yoo-NEEK*)
ADJECTIVE: Stands out; different.

uppish
(*UHP-ish*)
ADJECTIVE: Condescending; snooty.

uppishness
(*UHP-ish-nes*)
NOUN: To act in a way that is condescending or snooty.

> *Clyde's UPPISHNESS kept him from socializing with his coworkers since he considered himself to be on another level than they were.*

The proud man can learn

humility, but he will be

proud of it.

—Mignon McLaughlin

uppity
(*UHP-ih-tee*)
ADJECTIVE: Another word for uppish, meaning haughty and snooty.

vain
(*vayn*)
ADJECTIVE: Excessively proud of one's own self or actions.

vainglorious
(*vayn-GLAWR-ee-uhs*)
NOUN: Given to self-absorption; inclined to view oneself excessively or too highly.

vainglory
(*VAYN-glawr-ee*)
NOUN: Pride in one's own achievements.

vanity
(*VAN-ih-tee*)
NOUN: Excessive pride in oneself and one's own achievements.

vapor
(*VAY-per*)
VERB: To speak boastfully or pompously.

vaulting

(*VAWL-ting*)

ADJECTIVE: The act of leaping over something. Also, excessive ambition, as in *vaulting* pride.

vaunt

(*vawn*)

VERB: To excessively boast about something.

> *The couple's endless VAUNTING at the charity function was in extremely poor taste and caused many of the other people there to avoid entering into conversation with them.*

vaunter

(*VAWN-ter*)

NOUN: Someone who boasts excessively.

venerable

(*VEN-er-uh-buhl*)

ADJECTIVE: Commanding reverence; sacred.

ventosity

(*VEN-toh-sit-ee*)

NOUN: Speech that indicates inflated vanity. Literally windiness.

vouchsafe

(*vouch-SAYF*)

VERB: To deign or to condescend; to agree, in a condescending manner, to grant a request or do something; to offer as a favor or privilege.

W

Proud people breed sad

sorrows for themselves.

—EMILY BRONTE

wave off
(*wayv awf*)
VERB: To dismiss with a gesture; send away.

wealth
(*welth*)
NOUN: A great fortune.

weigh in
(*way in*)
VERB: To interject one's opinion into a conversation.

weight
(*wayt*)
NOUN: Importance or influence.

well-groomed
(*wel-groomd*)
ADJECTIVE: Neat and clean in appearance.

windbag
(*WIND-bag*)
NOUN: A person who talks on and on with the assumption that other people care what he or she is saying.

wise guy
(*wyz gy*)
NOUN: A person who acts like a know-it-all.

wiseacre

(*WYZ-ay-ker*)

NOUN: A know-it-all; one who professes to know everything.

wise-ass

(*WYZ-as*)

NOUN: A person who thinks that he or she is being clever.

> *While Martin is a sharp young man, his intellect and quick tongue make him quite the WISE-ASS, always making rude remarks whenever someone else is speaking.*

wisenheimer

(*WY-zuhn-hy-mer*)

NOUN: A person who acts in an arrogant manner; a know-it-all.

worthiness

(*WUR-thee-nes*)

NOUN: Deserving of respect or admiration.

wrapped up in oneself

(*rapd uhp in wuhn-SELF*)

PHRASE: A phrase meaning self-centered.

> *Katherine should have come to realize by now that she cannot speak to her husband about her problems because he is so WRAPPED UP IN HIMSELF he does not even listen to her.*

X, Y, and Z

yarn

(*yahrn*)

NOUN: A long account that has usually been exaggerated or fabricated to entertain the listener.

> *The boastful adventurer had no problem spinning quite the YARN about his most recent travels, greatly embellishing the details in order to impress his audience.*

yea-sayer

(*YAY-say-er*)

NOUN: A person who is positive in attitude.

yell

(*yel*)

VERB: To speak at a loud volume.

zenith

(*ZEE-nith*)

NOUN: The highest point; peak.